# GARDENING IS EASY
## when you know how

A
*Golden Hands*
book

Marshall Cavendish, London

**Author**
Diana Simmons

**Illustrations**
Marilyn Day

**Photographs**
Alan Duns

**Typography and Design**
Brian Liddle

**Editor**
Karen Harriman

Published by Marshall Cavendish Publications Ltd,
58, Old Compton Street,
London, W1V 5PA

ISBN 0 85685 073 X

This volume first printed 1974

Printed by Ben Johnson & Company Ltd., York,
England

This edition not to be sold in the U.S.A. Canada
or the Philippines

# About This Book

So you would like a garden of your own?

Maybe it will be only a pot on a window-sill or—if you are lucky—a small plot in your parents' garden. Whatever you grow, in a pot or plot, will be all your own creation—with a little help from nature.

Plants and flowers need almost as much care as your pets or yourself! We all need light, air, food and water, for healthy growth . . . and so will your plants. Whether you grow beautiful plants, or tasty things to eat, indoors or outdoors, you are going to have lots of fun gardening.

As you watch your first seedlings grow, day by day, you will realize that gardening is a fascinating and rewarding hobby.

# Contents

# Root-Top Gardens

## You Will Need

Several root vegetables
A large plate
Some clean pebbles

The tops of root vegetables like carrots, turnips, parsnips and beetroots [beets] are usually thrown away. Save some to make a very pretty garden which will grow quickly.

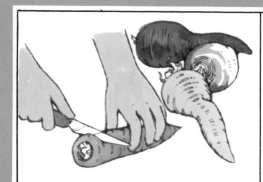

**1** The root vegetables your mother buys in the shops have probably already had their leaves removed. So ask her to give you some and slice 1.3 cm (½ in.) from the top of each one.

**2** If the vegetables have been dug up from the garden, trim the leaves, leaving about a 6 mm (¼ in.) of stem on the slice you cut.

**3** Put the root-tops on a large plate with just enough water to cover the bottom.

**4** To add interest, fill the gaps between the root-tops with some clean pebbles.

**5** Put the plate on a sunny window-sill. In a few days, you will see the tiny shoots starting to grow.

**6** Growing plants need plenty of water, so keep your garden well watered. In two or three weeks you will have a lovely leafy garden.

# Mustard and Cress

You can begin your gardening by sowing mustard and cress which grows very quickly. You will enjoy eating it all the more because you have grown it yourself!

## You Will Need

Dinner plates

Several squares of absorbent kitchen paper

A packet each of mustard and cress seeds

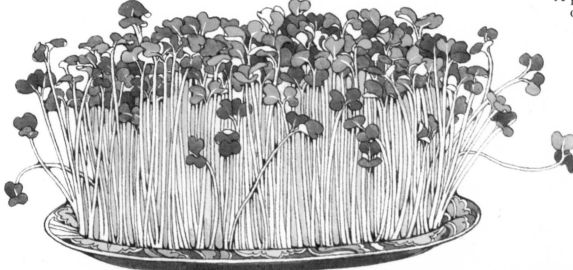

**1** Place the paper on a dinner plate and wet it well with water. Pour away the excess water.

**2** Sprinkle some cress seeds quite thinly on one half of the paper, making sure no seeds lie on top of each other.

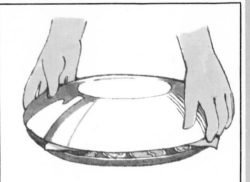

**3** Cover your seeds with a dry square of paper or place another plate over the top, to keep out the light until the tiny roots and shoots start to grow.

**4** Three days later, sow the mustard seeds on the other half of the paper. Mustard germinates more quickly than cress, so they will be ready to cut at the same time. Keep the paper moist but not soaking wet. Cover again.

**5** When the cress is about 1.3 cm ($\frac{1}{2}$ in.) high, uncover and place the plate on a sunny window-sill. Don't forget to keep the paper moist. Let your crop grow to about 7.5 cm (3 in.) high when it will be ready to harvest.

**6** Cut with scissors and eat in sandwiches or salad. If your family likes your home-grown salad keep up the supply! One packet of both mustard and cress seeds will give several crops.

# Know-how for Indoor Gardening

**Compost** [Potting mixture]

This is a special mixture of soil, peat and sand which contains all the food plants need for healthy growth. It is used especially for growing plants indoors in pots. A pot plant grows in very little soil, so this must be really nourishing and able to absorb water yet drain well. Some garden soils can harden in a small pot and will prevent the water from draining through properly.

**Fertiliser**

Fertiliser is a rich plant food, which acts as a tonic for plants when their roots and shoots are growing quickly. Liquid fertilisers are the easiest to use. Read the bottle carefully to find out the right amount to use.

**When to water**

Most plants need more water in spring and summer when they are growing fast and are in flower than they do in winter when they are resting. (Plants that flower in winter need more water at this time than summer-flowering plants.) Outside, the natural rainfall is usually enough to supply the plants with all the water they need, except in really hot, dry weather. Inside, they need more attention. If the soil in the pot falls off your finger when you touch it, it is time to water your plant. If it sticks to your finger, the soil is damp enough.

**Watering Pot Plants**

Make sure your plant pot is standing in a drip saucer before watering. Pour water on to the soil in the pot until you see it has drained through to the saucer. The plant will drink up the water through its roots.

## Taking Cuttings From House Plants

You can use cuttings from house plants in the bottle and plate gardens.

STEM CUTTINGS

## You Will Need

A pair of scissors

A plant with plenty of strong shoots

A jar of water or a pot of compost [potting mixture]

Choose a healthy plant with plenty of strong shoots. Select one of the shoots and with the scissors cut it off just below a leaf joint to give you a cutting about 10 cm (4 in.) long. This joint where the leaf is or was attached to the stem is a tiny bud from which new roots and shoots will grow.

Some plants are easier than others to grow from cuttings. Cuttings from Tradescantia, Coleus, Philodendron scandens, Busy Lizzie, Ivies and Peperomias will take root particularly easily. These plants will root in water or compost [potting mixture].

## OFF-SETS

Some plants produce their own 'baby' plants. Spider plant and Mother of Thousands are two. These little plantlets can be cut off and planted in pots or used directly in the bottle, plate and water gardens.

## LEAF CUTTINGS

Sometimes a new plant will grow from a single leaf or a portion of a leaf. An African Violet leaf and stem can be planted in a pot. When the new plants are big enough to grow on their own the same leaf can be used again to act as a parent.

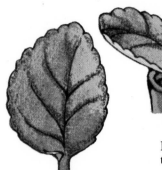

Pick leaves with stalks and put several in the same pot of compost [potting mixture].

When you see clusters of tiny new leaves you can move the new plants into small, individual pots.

# Stocking up Outdoors

Friends and neighbours may be happy to help you to stock your garden with plants, by giving you cuttings and roots from their plants.

## HEEL CUTTINGS

Take off a side shoot from a shrub or a bush. Slice it off with a piece of the main stem.

To help the new roots grow quickly, dip the cutting in a special hormone rooting powder you can buy.

Put your cutting in a pot of compost [potting mixture], or outside, wherever you want it to grow.

## DIVIDING ONE PLANT TO MAKE OTHERS

Bulbs and plants with fibrous roots, like Michaelmas daisies, can be divided.

Dig the plant up.

Pull off some side shoots with roots attached and re-plant them in your garden.

Bulbs, like daffodils and tulips, produce small 'daughter' bulb off-sets which can be broken away from the main bulb and grown for a new crop.

# Fun with Citrus Fruit Pips

Think how proud you would be to grow tiny trees from fruit pips. Orange, lemon, grapefruit, mandarin and tangerine pips will grow easily, especially when started off in the spring.

## You Will Need

Citrus pips

1 flower pot filled with compost [potting mixture]

Several small pots filled with compost [potting mixture]

**1** Take your pips from fruit with plenty in them. Fill a flower pot with compost [potting mixture], water it well and press in two or three pips just under the soil.

**2** Do not forget to label your pots, to be sure which plant is which when they start to grow.

**3** Keep the pots in a warm, dark place until you can see the first shoot. An airing cupboard is a good place. The pips will take several weeks to germinate. Meanwhile keep the compost [potting mixture] moist.

**4** Transfer the pots to a sunny window-sill. When the plants have grown two pairs of leaves, carefully transplant them into their own little pots.

**5** In a few months you will have little trees with shiny, dark green leaves and, if you care for them for several years, you may even get some lovely scented blossom and tiny fruit!

## Amaze your friends with these plants

### THE COFFEE PLANT (Coffea)

The coffee plant can be grown from seed into a pretty evergreen pot-plant. It has clusters of cream, perfumed flowers, followed by crimson berries. Each berry contains two coffee beans. The coffee beans must be roasted before they can be used to make coffee.

### BURNING BUSH (Kochia)

Burning bush is an interesting plant for your garden. It looks like a little pine tree with narrow, feathery leaves. The exciting time is in late summer when the Burning bush turns deep red. You can grow these bushes from seeds, starting them off in the garden in spring.

### AUTUMN CROCUS (Colchicum)

This is a fascinating bulb with several other names—'naked ladies', 'meadow saffron'. It can be grown without soil or water. Buy a bulb in late summer, put it in a saucer and watch it flower. The tall, broad leaves will follow much later in early spring. It will only flower for you once in this way, but if you put it in the garden, it will flower again in time.

# Tropical Treasures

## You Will Need

1 pineapple
1 pot sand
3 date stones
1 pot compost [potting mixture]

## Dates and Pineapples

These fruits grow naturally in hot countries, so do not attempt to grow them unless you can give them a great deal of warmth.

**1** Slice the top from a pineapple, including as little of the flesh as possible. Lie it on its side and let the air reach the cut side for a few days. Plant it in a pot of damp sand.

**2** The date stone can be planted straight into a pot of moist compost [potting mixture]. Plant two or three stones to avoid disappointment.

**5** Move the pineapple to a pot full of compost [potting mixture] when its roots are growing well. Put this in a warm place. If you can keep it in a tropically heated greenhouse your pineapple plant could even produce pineapple!

**3** Slip your planted pots into clear plastic bags and tie the tops tightly, so that no air can get inside. Put the plastic bags in a really warm place—an airing cupboard, on top of a radiator, or in a heated greenhouse. Look at your plants every week or two, to check that the soil is still moist.

**4** When you see shoots sprouting from your date stones you can bring them out but keep them in a warm spot. Keep them inside their plastic bags until they each have three leaves. Carefully transfer them to their own pots, where they will grow into leafy palms.

10

# Avocado Pears

Inside an avocado pear fruit is a large stone, which you can grow easily to produce a charming plant. You can start to grow your avocado pear in two ways: in a pot of compost [potting mixture], or in water which is more fun as you can watch its progress.

## You Will Need

1 avocado stone
1 glass jar
2 match sticks
1 pot filled with compost
  [potting mixture]

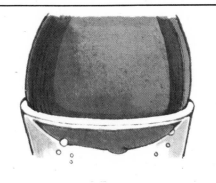

**1** Soak the stone in water for a day or two so it will germinate more quickly.

**2** Now put the stone in the neck of a glass jar which is almost full of water. The large end of the stone should be just touching the water. Support the stone with match sticks.

**3** After a few weeks the stone will start to split and you will see a shoot and root appearing.

**4** When there are plenty of strong roots, transfer the plant to a pot of compost [potting mixture]. It should cover half of the stone.

**5** Avocados can grow very tall. If you want a large plant remember to transplant it to a larger pot when it outgrows the first one. It may need supporting with a stick as it grows taller to keep the stem straight.

11

# Cacti Collection

## You Will Need

A seed tray

Compost [potting mixture]

Coarse sand

A packet of mixed cacti seeds
   or a number of small cacti

A shallow container

Pebbles or charcoal

A small hand mirror

Toy camels

In a desert, cacti can grow as tall as buildings, but indoors they grow very slowly, so they are easy to control. Their strange shapes and prickly spines will make a very interesting garden. You can buy them in tiny pots, grow them from a mixed packet of seeds or adopt 'baby' off-shoots from friends' plants. Growing cacti from seed needs lots of patience but it is worthwhile as you will get a number of varieties for a small outlay. The seeds need heat to start them germinating. So wait until the weather is warm if you do not have a warm place in which to keep them.

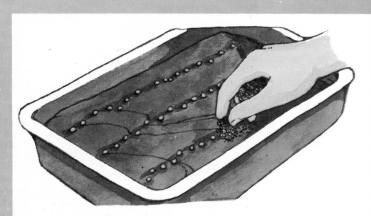

**1** Fill a seed tray with a mixture of compost [potting mixture] and coarse sand. Sprinkle the seeds evenly over the surface and cover with a very light layer of compost [potting mixture]. Water the soil and cover the tray.

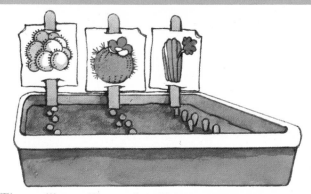

**2** The seedlings will grow best if they are left in the seed tray for a year. Water them regularly to keep the compost [potting mixture] damp. It is fascinating to watch them grow and see what comes up. Don't forget to keep your seed packet to help you identify the cacti as they appear.

**3** Prepare your desert plate with a layer of pebbles or charcoal for drainage. Fill up the container with a mixture of compost [potting mixture] and sand. Sprinkle a fine layer of sand over the top to make it look like a real desert.

**4** Plant your cacti about 10 cm (4 in.) apart. To make an 'oasis' in your desert, place a small hand mirror by a tall cactus with a few model camels grouped around it as shown in the picture opposite.

# Plate Gardens

Miniature gardens are lots of fun. You can grow a real lawn and keep it neat with nail scissors. You could make a lake from a tin lid, painted blue and filled with water. Then you can add a bridge and a duck to float on your lake. Use your imagination. You can include almost anything as long as it is small and in proportion with the rest of your garden.

14

# You Will Need

A shallow container like a baking tin, a tin tray, or a large plate

Pebbles or charcoal

Compost [potting mixture]

Plants—choose from: SNOW-DROPS, DWARF CYCLAMENS, CROCUS, SCILLA and DWARF ALPINE PLANTS like SAXIFRAGE, THYME, SEDUM and THRIFT

Finest quality grass seed or moss

Dwarf conifer

Fine gravel

Small stones

Toy animals

Plastic bottle with spray nozzle

**1** Spread a thin layer of pebbles or charcoal in your dish or tray to absorb water.

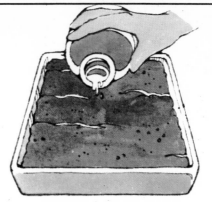

**2** Fill up the dish or tray with compost [potting mixture] and water it well before you start planting.

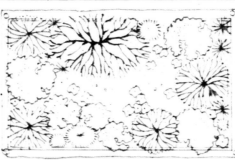

**3** Draw the plan of your miniature garden on a piece of paper first. Then you can decide where everything should go. As you plant the garden remember to leave room for the plants to grow and spread.

**4** Use an old spoon as a spade and dig small holes for bulbs and plants. If the plant's roots are deeper than the plate, shake off the soil and spread out the roots.

**5** Cuttings can be gently pressed in with your fingers. Press the soil firmly round all your plants.

**6** Seeds should be spread sparingly on the soil and lightly covered with a sprinkling of compost [potting mixture].

**7** If you want a lawn, sow the finest quality grass seed or use moss. If you would like a tree, choose an evergreen. Many dwarf conifers grow very slowly.

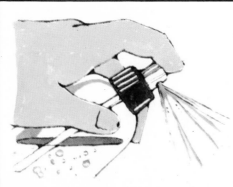

**8** Once the garden is planted never let it dry out. Each day you should spray the plants with water, using a clean plastic bottle with a spray nozzle.

**9** If possible, put the garden outside during the summer months. Indoors, it should be kept near the window.

**10** If some of your plants outgrow the garden, dig them up and divide them into pieces, returning some to your plate garden and using others to start a new one.

# Bottle Garden

Bottle gardens are fun for everybody, especially lazy gardeners! Once they are planted you can leave them to grow with very little attention.

## Making Tools

## You Will Need

A kitchen fork and spoon

Thin bamboo canes

Paper

Sticky tape

2 thin sticks or a pair of chopsticks

Small piece of foam sponge

Cotton reel [spool]

Wire

Pins

A large glass bottle—a carboy; a gallon-sized wine or cider flagon or a large candy jar

Charcoal

Compost [potting mixture]

Your home-made tools

Plants.

**1** Lash a kitchen fork and spoon to bamboo canes to make useful miniature garden tools for moving the soil and firming in your plants. **2** Use the paper to make a cone. Cut out a half circle and fold it into a cone shape, sticking the sides together with sticky tape. Cut off the pointed bottom. You now have a funnel through which you will pour the soil into your bottle. **3** You can use two thin sticks or a pair of chopsticks like tweezers to gently lower plants into position. **4** Attach a cotton reel [spool] to a bamboo cane and use it to press the roots firmly into the soil when planting. **5** Fix a small piece of foam sponge on to a length of flexible wire for mopping away moisture and cleaning the soil from the inside of the bottle after planting. **6** Make a spiked tool by taping four pins round the end of a bamboo cane to pick up dead leaves and flower heads.

17

There are many plants which will grow well in your bottle garden. Do not use fully grown plants. Take leaf and stem cuttings where you can and add some young plants.

**African violet** (Saintpaulia)
This plant, with its purple, pink or white flowers, stays in flower for months. You can grow a new plant from just one leaf.

**Snake-skin plant** (Sansevieria)
This is a plant with delicate, silver-veined leaves. It is a creeper and will grow low.

**Pepper elder** (Peperomia)
This plant had fleshy, heart-shaped leaves. There are several varieties, with unusual markings and colours. The variety *caperata variegata* has green and white crinkly leaves and cream flower spikes with red stems.

**Mother-in-law's tongue** (Fittonia)
The dark green sword-like leaves of this plant with their smart golden markings are very striking. You can grow a new plant from a single leaf.

**Maidenhair fern** (Adiantum)
This plant has delicate, pale green sprays of leaves on thin black stems.

**Wandering Jew** (Tradescantia or Zebrina)
These two plants are very similar in appearance. They have pretty, striped, pointed leaves on long trailing stems.

**Spider plant** (Chlorophytum)
This is a lovely green and white striped plant with grassy leaves. It produces lots of miniature plants on the end of slender arching stems.

# Planting the Bottle Garden

**1** Wash and dry your bottle thoroughly before you start. If it is not dry the soil will stick to the sides. Put your paper funnel in the neck of the bottle and pour in a layer of charcoal chips.

**5** Press the roots firmly in place with your cotton reel [spool] tool.

18

**2** Fill up with compost [potting mixture] until bottle is one-third full.

**3** Plan your planting so that tall plants are at the back, leaving room for the low creeping plants to carpet the floor of the bottle. Remember to leave spaces between the plants so they have room to grow.

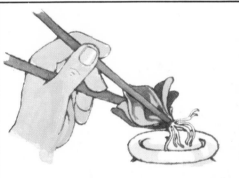

**4** Now comes the tricky part! Use your spoon tool to dig a planting hole. Gently fold together the leaves of a plant and lower it into the bottle, using two thin sticks or a pair of chopsticks.

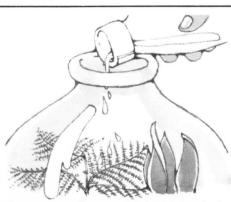

**6** When you have finished planting, trickle in tepid water until the compost [potting mixture] is thoroughly damp but not soggy.

**7** Clean the inside of the glass bottle, where the soil has splattered against the sides, using your tiny sponge on its flexible wire handle.

**8** If you have a screw top or cork to use as a stopper, put it into the neck of the bottle to keep in the moisture. Stand your bottle garden in a light place, but not in strong sunlight.

# Underwater Gardens

An underwater garden makes an attractive home for goldfish and an interesting garden project for you. It is great fun to watch the fish swimming around the plants and to study how the plants grow underwater. Water snails will help to keep your tank clean but if it does turn green allow it to clear by itself. Thin out the plants in the tank when they get too thick.

## You Will Need

A fish tank about 37.5 by 30 cm (15 by 12 in.)

Sand

Garden soil or compost [potting mixture]

Clean water

Plants—choose from:
BOG ARUM; PONDWEED;
FAIRY MOSS; WATER FRINGE

Clean stones

Pebbles and shells

A pair of goldfish and a few water snails

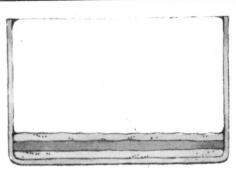

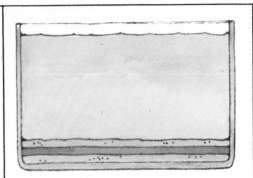

**1** Make a sandwich of 2.5 cm (1 in.) of garden soil or compost [potting mixture] between two 2.5 cm (1 in.) layers of sand to cover the bottom of the tank.

**2** Fill the tank with clean water and leave the sand to settle until the water clears.

**3** Plant the tank, putting the tallest plants at the back. Gently push the roots through the top layer of sand into the soil. Place a few stones around the stems to stop the plants floating to the surface.

**4** Decorate the sand with shells and pebbles. If you have collected them from a beach, remember to wash off all the salt first.

**5** Now add one or two floating plants; the other plants will like their shadow.

**6** Let your plants take root before adding the fish and the water snails. Water snails will not need feeding, but goldfish will need regular food. However, be careful not to over do it, because this can make the water smell unpleasant.

21

# Plants in Pebbles

Many plants will grow quite happily in pebbles and water without soil. They will not grow as large but, if you plant several together in a water-tight container, you can make a lovely leafy garden.

## You Will Need

An attractive container like a lidless teapot; a jumbo-size cup and saucer; a glass bowl (so you can see the roots growing)

Charcoal

Small pebbles, gravel and shells

Plants—choose from:
**MOTHER OF THOUSANDS** (Saxifraga sarmentosa)
**WANDERING JEW** (Tradescantia)
**SPIDER PLANT** (Chlorophytum)
**BUSY LIZZIE** (Impatiens)
**FLAME NETTLE** (Coleus)

A bottle of liquid plant food

**1** Prepare your container by first covering the bottom with charcoal. Then add a layer of pebbles.

**2** Plant your garden with stem cuttings taken from the parent plant. You can start off your cuttings in individual glass jars and let them grow there, until you can see the new roots. Or you can put your cuttings straight into the water garden.

**3** Put the plants into the container with the trailers round the edge and the upright ones in the middle.

**4** Support the stems with pebbles and shells. The pebbles should reach up to the rim of the container. When the garden is planted fill up the container with water.

**5** As your plants grow some of the trailers may get out of hand. Keep cutting them back and use the pieces to start more gardens.

**6** Keep filling up the water level. When the roots are growing really well, you can begin to feed the plants with a weak solution of liquid plant food, about once a month.

**7** In warm weather, if the water becomes warm, run the container under the cold tap to aerate the plants' roots.

# Window Boxes for all seasons

Whether you live in a house, a flat or an apartment, a window-box can make a perfect miniature garden which will look pretty all through the year.

## You Will Need

A window-box
Plants
Pebbles
Charcoal pieces
Peat, turf or leaf soil
Compost [potting mixture]

**1** Fill a window-box with a layer of pebbles. Cover each drainage hole with one large piece of pebble.

**2** Add some charcoal to keep the soil sweet. Then add some rough material like peat, turf or leaf soil.

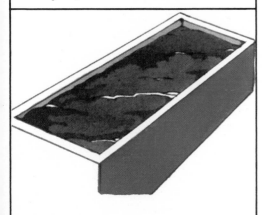

**3** Fill up the box with compost [potting mixture]. Your window-box is now ready for planting.

SPRING   Bulbs grow easily in window-boxes. If the window-box is in a windy place, choose the dwarf varieties. Plant your spring-flowering bulbs in the autumn. Put daffodils, hyacinths and tulips at the back and crocus, scilla and grape hyacinth in front. When they have finished flowering, you can plant your summer collection. Keep one or two dwarf evergreen shrubs to give you greenery all through the year.

SUMMER   There are many annuals which you can grow from seed for your window-box. Start these off in seed trays in the spring, so they will be ready to plant out when you lift your bulbs. When choosing your seeds remember you will need some edging plants like allyssum and lobelia. Ageratum, pansy, petunia and nasturtium are all good value to rear from seed. They will flower all summer long.
AUTUMN AND WINTER   If your box looks bare as autumn progresses, plant a few variegated ivies trailing over the edge to help fill up the gaps until the spring bulbs start growing.

23

# Hanging Baskets

A hanging garden will look very pretty suspended from a hook on the porch outside your front door especially if you choose brightly coloured plants and creepers.

## You Will Need

A strong wire basket at least 30.5 cm (12 in.) in diameter— the larger the basket, the better the effect will be

A bucket

Moss and peat

Compost [potting mixture]

Plants

**1** Stand the basket on something steady like a bucket.

**2** Line the bottom with a thick layer of fresh damp moss and peat to help retain moisture.

**3** Fill up the basket with compost [potting mixture]. Scoop out a shallow hole in the centre to collect water.

**4** Plant about three or four large plants and a similar number of smaller, trailing ones in your basket.

**5** Fill up the sides with little trailers like lobelia, nasturtiums, tradescantia.

**6** When you have finished planting, thoroughly soak the basket by immersing it in water. Do not hang it up until it is well drained. During the summer, when it needs watering, it should be soaked again in water.

# Hanging baskets are lovely in a porch or on a balcony

Don't forget to take off dead flower heads to encourage more flowers to grow.

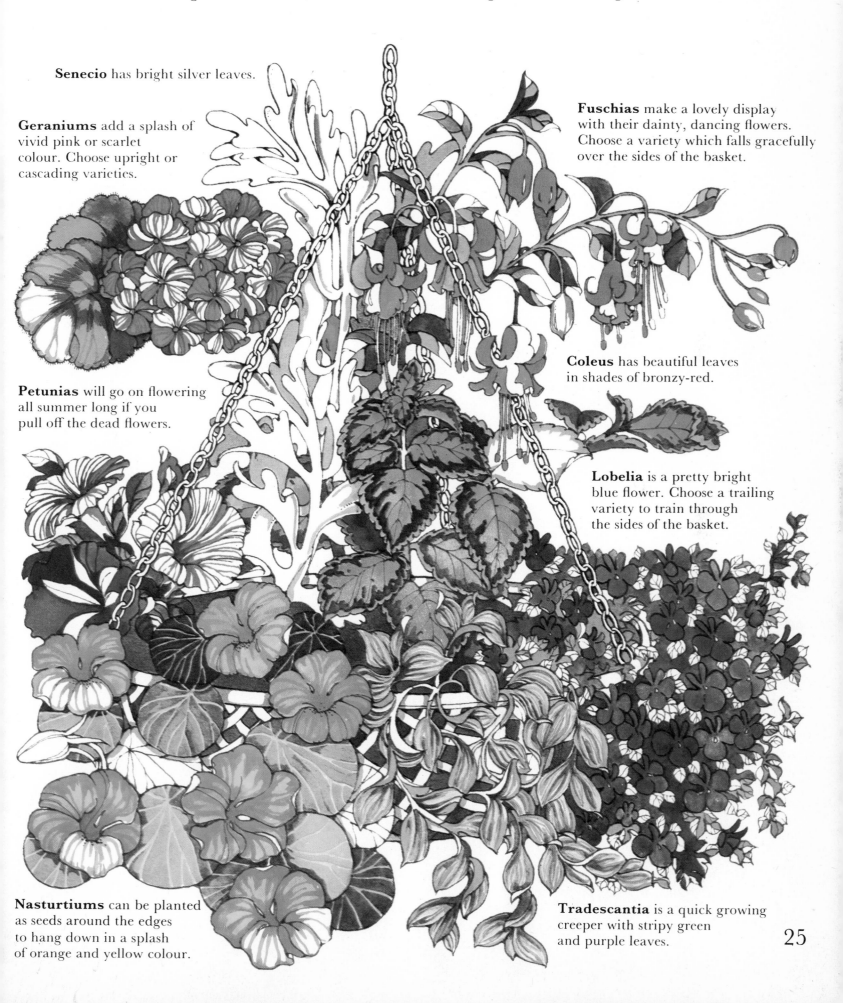

**Senecio** has bright silver leaves.

**Geraniums** add a splash of vivid pink or scarlet colour. Choose upright or cascading varieties.

**Fuschias** make a lovely display with their dainty, dancing flowers. Choose a variety which falls gracefully over the sides of the basket.

**Coleus** has beautiful leaves in shades of bronzy-red.

**Petunias** will go on flowering all summer long if you pull off the dead flowers.

**Lobelia** is a pretty bright blue flower. Choose a trailing variety to train through the sides of the basket.

**Nasturtiums** can be planted as seeds around the edges to hang down in a splash of orange and yellow colour.

**Tradescantia** is a quick growing creeper with stripy green and purple leaves.

# Preparing an Outside Garden

Perhaps you will be lucky enough to have a small plot in your parents' garden in which you will enjoy growing flowers and vegetables. It will produce better plants if you prepare it properly. The earth, unlike the compost [potting mixture] you have been using, will have weeds and stones in it. The ground may be hard after the winter and will need digging to make it soft. Preparing your garden well, for the growing season, will ensure healthy plants.

**1** Pull out all the weeds, making sure that you can recognize a weed from a plant.

**2** Dig out common weeds like nettle, ground elder, bindweed and thistle with their roots otherwise they will grow again very quickly. These weeds are all perennials which means they will come up each year.

**3** Pull up annual weeds like groundsel, chickweed and speedwell when they are young. They will not grow again if you take them out of the ground before they flower and make seeds.

**4** Dig your garden with a spade or fork.

**5** Take out any large stones, as the little roots will not be able to get around them. Leave very small stones, they help to let air into the soil and improve drainage.

**6** Rake the soil to make it crumbly and pick up any more big stones or weeds turned up by the rake.

27

# Your Friends and

There are many poisons to kill garden pests, but they can be dangerous if not used properly. Also, they may kill those small creatures which can help your garden. So it is better to help nature a little and try to remove some of the 'foes' yourself without using dangerous chemicals. Encourage the helpful predators in your garden to help you get rid of some of the 'foes'.

**Ladybirds** and their grubs feed on greenfly.

**Centipedes,** which have one pair of legs to each segment of their bodies, can benefit the garden. Their favourite foods are insect larvae, slugs and snails.

## FRIENDS

**Frogs** and **toads** would be happy if you have a water garden. Their diet includes caterpillars, woodlice, slugs and insects.

**Ground beetles** feed on insects and slugs.

**Earthworms** wriggle and tunnel so much they let air into the soil. They eat plant matter like dead leaves which they draw below ground. This helps to enrich the soil.
The colour of an earthworm will also tell you about the type of soil in which it lives. If the worm is very pale the soil is likely to be waterlogged or poor quality. If it is dark red it means the soil is rich and well drained.

# Foes in the Garden

You could trap slugs under half an orange or grapefruit skin. Lay the skin on the ground, round side upwards, to make a little house. Cut a piece from the edge to make an entrance. Look under it each day for 'prisoners' and take them out of harm's way.

## FOES

**Slugs** and **snails** feed on vegetation and come into the garden for their meals because many wild plants have developed hairy leaves and stems and the garden plants do not have the same protection. If you find snails in your garden, move them somewhere where they will do no harm.

**Millipedes** have two pairs of legs on each segment. They will eat the roots of vegetables and bulbs. You can trap them in a hollowed-out turnip.

**Aphids** — 'greenfly' and 'blackfly' — will quickly spread on a plant. You must ask an adult for help in getting rid of them, since the plant must be sprayed with a chemical.

**Woodlice** can be similarly trapped with hollowed-out apples.

**Caterpillars** eat leaves, making small holes in them. If you see their yellow eggs on the underside of leaves, you should destroy them.

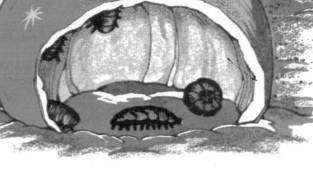

# Flowers for picking

When all the hard work of preparing your plot is over, you will want to grow some flowers to show colourful results quickly. These flowers are hardy annuals and will survive most weather from early spring to autumn. They can be sown straight into your garden and will flower all through the summer.

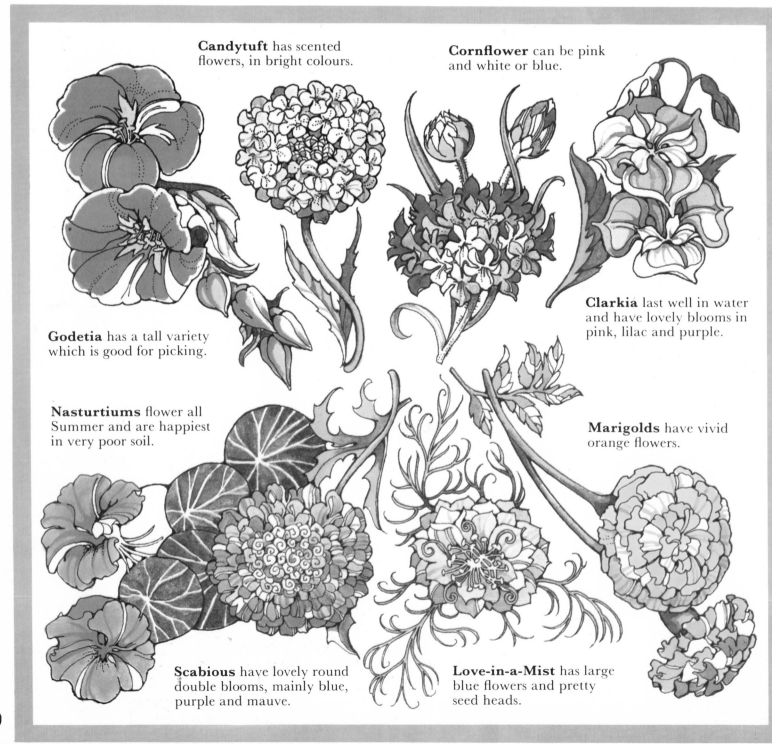

**Candytuft** has scented flowers, in bright colours.

**Cornflower** can be pink and white or blue.

**Godetia** has a tall variety which is good for picking.

**Clarkia** last well in water and have lovely blooms in pink, lilac and purple.

**Nasturtiums** flower all Summer and are happiest in very poor soil.

**Marigolds** have vivid orange flowers.

**Scabious** have lovely round double blooms, mainly blue, purple and mauve.

**Love-in-a-Mist** has large blue flowers and pretty seed heads.

30

**1** Plant your seeds in the spring. Rake the earth to make it very fine.

**2** The day before sowing, water the soil gently with the fine spray on your watering can.

**3** Sprinkle the seeds thinly and lightly rake over some soil to cover them.

**4** When the seedlings are about 2.5 cm (1 in.) high, thin them out by pulling some out to leave the others more room to grow.

**5** As the plants grow, some of the tall ones may need to be tied against a stick to support them.

**6** Now in early summer you can take your mother her first bunch of flowers!

# Gather your own seeds

Make your own collection of seeds from the garden which you can keep and plant for next year's crop.

Gather the seeds from flowers when they have finished flowering. The easiest seeds to gather are those in pods such as lupins, wallflowers, honesty and broom.

Vegetables, like beans and peas, can also be stored to use the following year. Take the seeds from the pods and put them in envelopes, using a separate one for each different plant. Label each envelope carefully with the name of the plant from which the seeds came. Store the envelope in a cool, dry, airy place during the winter. In the spring you will be able to sow the seeds in your garden.

# Growing Herbs

A pot of your own herbs would be a welcome present for any cook. Many are easy to grow, either in pots of compost [potting mixture] or in your garden. Here are some of the most popular for kitchen use.

## Parsley

Parsley can be grown from seed. Sow the seeds thinly in spring. Soak them in warm water the day before you sow. This will help the seeds germinate more quickly. When your plant is growing well, keep cutting the leaves for cooking and to encourage the plant to grow. Fresh parsley is used in white sauce and to garnish vegetables.

## Chives

Chives grow well in pots. You will need a small clump, divided from a plant in spring. When it is established, you should cut and use the leaves frequently to keep it growing well. Water it often if it is in a pot. Chives have a delicate onion flavour and are used, finely chopped, in salads, mixed with cream cheese and in egg dishes.

## Sage

Sage is a spreading shrub and cuttings can be taken in spring or summer. The leaves can be used, fresh or dried, to flavour meat and in stuffings.

## Rosemary

Rosemary is a pretty shrub and you can grow a new plant from a cutting taken in late summer. Rosemary has a strong spicy flavour and is delicious with roast lamb and chicken.

## Mint

Mint spreads rapidly, so if you are growing it in your garden, confine it to one spot by planting it in a large can with both ends removed. You can start a new crop in the spring, by cutting up some pieces of root and planting them. Mint is used in mint sauce and served with lamb.

## Thyme

Thyme is a low spreading plant. A cutting with a piece of root or a small piece, divided from a large plant, can start off a new plant in spring. Thyme has a strong flavour and a little goes a long way in stews, soups and stuffing.

# Drying Herbs to use in the Kitchen

If your herb garden is growing well and you have some herbs to spare, you can preserve them to use in the kitchen through the winter.

Harvest the herbs on a dry sunny day, when the plants are flowering.

Tie them in small bunches.

Hang them in a warm place to dry. When they are dry, the leaves will feel brittle and stems will snap easily.

Take off the leaves and crumble them between your hands.

Put the different herbs in separate air-tight glass jars.

Make your own pretty labels for each one.

MINT

SAGE

THYME

Parsl

VES

# Salad Bowl

During a hot summer, fresh salad vegetables are very welcome. You can grow your own salad bowl. Vegetables like a richer soil than flowers, so dig in fertiliser or manure if possible.

## You Will Need

A rake
A packet of radish seeds
A spade

## Radishes

**1** Rake the soil to remove any lumps and stones.

**2** Sow the seeds sparingly about 1.3 cm (½ in.) deep. Space them out if you can, to save thinning them later. This is easy if you buy 'pelleted' seeds.

**3** Cover the seeds with a light sprinkling of soil and pat it down firmly with the back of a spade.

**4** You can continue sowing every three weeks until mid-summer.

**5** Your first crop will be ready to pull up about three weeks after sowing.

**6** Ask your mother to cut them into 'flowers' to put in the salad bowl.

## Lettuce

A crisp lettuce in the salad bowl will be enjoyed by the family. If you keep pets which eat green leaves, grow some for them too.

## You Will Need

A packet of lettuce seeds

**1** Start sowing lettuce seeds in early spring.

**2** If you want lettuce all summer, sow a few seeds every two weeks until the mid-summer.

34

**3** Thin out the plants to 15 cm (6 in.) apart.

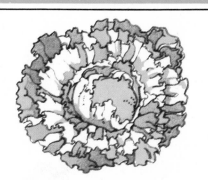

**4** When the hearts are full your lettuce are ready to cut. Cut them in the early morning while the dew is still on them.

**5** Now you, your family and your pets can eat them.

# Cucumbers

## You Will Need

A spade
A packet of cucumber seeds
Jam jar
Watering can with a fine spray
Liquid plant food

Cucumbers can be grown easily in the garden; they like living on a little ridge of soil. Remember to choose an outdoor variety when you buy your packet of seeds.

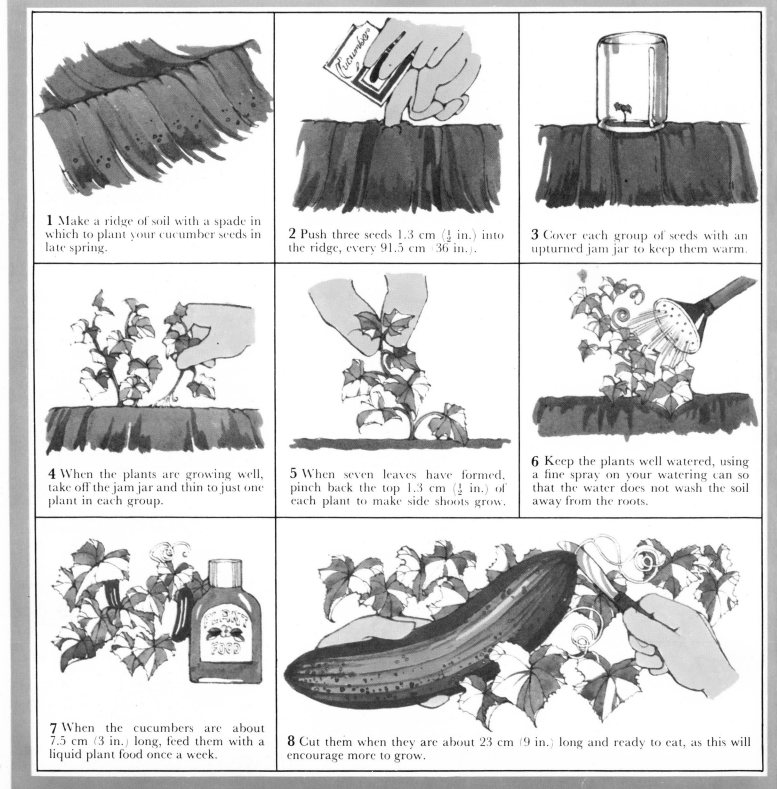

**1** Make a ridge of soil with a spade in which to plant your cucumber seeds in late spring.

**2** Push three seeds 1.3 cm ($\frac{1}{2}$ in.) into the ridge, every 91.5 cm (36 in.).

**3** Cover each group of seeds with an upturned jam jar to keep them warm.

**4** When the plants are growing well, take off the jam jar and thin to just one plant in each group.

**5** When seven leaves have formed, pinch back the top 1.3 cm ($\frac{1}{2}$ in.) of each plant to make side shoots grow.

**6** Keep the plants well watered, using a fine spray on your watering can so that the water does not wash the soil away from the roots.

**7** When the cucumbers are about 7.5 cm (3 in.) long, feed them with a liquid plant food once a week.

**8** Cut them when they are about 23 cm (9 in.) long and ready to eat, as this will encourage more to grow.

# A Potful of Tomatoes

## You Will Need

A packet of dwarf bush tomato seeds

Plant pots

Compost [potting mixture]

Liquid plant food

A dwarf bush of tomatoes, producing delicious miniature fruit, can be grown in a pot on a window-sill or in a sheltered spot in the garden.

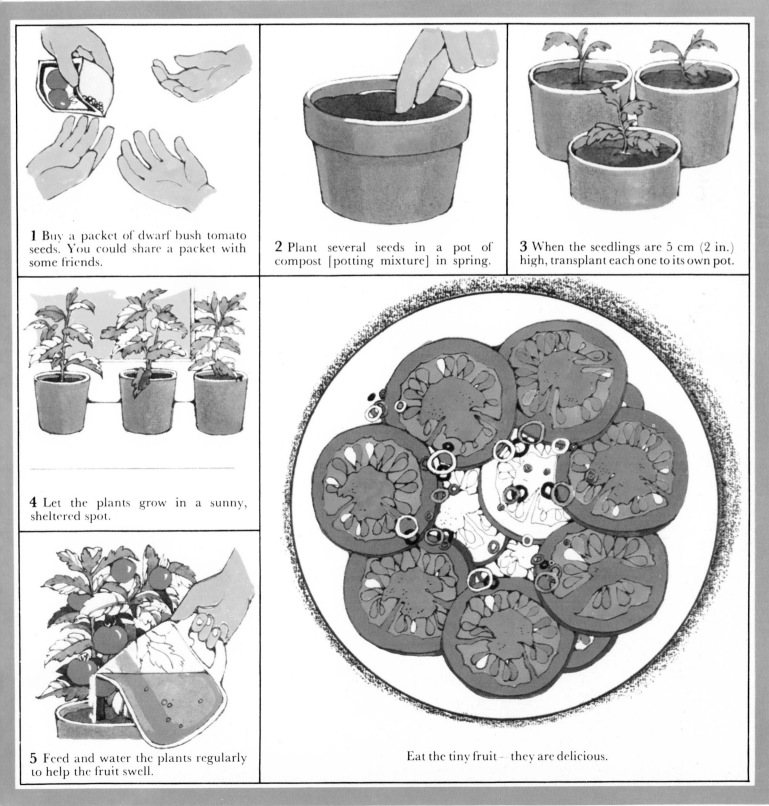

**1** Buy a packet of dwarf bush tomato seeds. You could share a packet with some friends.

**2** Plant several seeds in a pot of compost [potting mixture] in spring.

**3** When the seedlings are 5 cm (2 in.) high, transplant each one to its own pot.

**4** Let the plants grow in a sunny, sheltered spot.

**5** Feed and water the plants regularly to help the fruit swell.

Eat the tiny fruit – they are delicious.

# Fun with Flowers

It is fun to plant your name and see it grow day by day. For a flower name choose Virginia Stock, or for an 'edible name' mustard and cress.

## Plant Your Name

## You Will Need

A stick
A packet of seed
A flat board

**1** Trace your name in the soil with a stick.

**2** Sprinkle the seeds along the line of your name. Remember if you are growing mustard and cress seeds, sow the cress three days before the mustard.

**3** Do not cover the seeds with soil. Just press them gently into the ground with a flat board.

**4** Watch your name grow and flower. If you planted mustard and cress, now is the time to eat your name!

**5** If your father is growing marrows [summer squash] cut your name lightly into one while it is very small.

**6** As the marrow [summer squash] grows so will the size of your name.

## Games

Have a Sunflower race with your friends to see who can grow the tallest. Sunflowers can grow from 2 to 3 metres (6 to 10 feet) and sometimes even taller!

**1** Buy a packet of giant sunflower seeds (*Helianthus*). Divide them equally among your friends.

**2** Decide which day you will all sow the seeds. Choose a really sunny spot and sow the seeds about 60 cm (24 in.) apart, as they like plenty of room to grow.

**3** Water them throughout the summer to help them grow.

**4** Sunflowers grow very, very fast. Have a tall stick ready to support each plant as it develops.

**5** Fix your judging date for some time in late summer and decide on a prize for the winner.

**6** Save the flower heads after the race. You can keep the seeds for next year's competition. There will be plenty over for birds, who love to peck the seeds from the flower heads.

# Flowers to Dry and Keep

Some flowers are especially suitable for drying and preserving. Here are some you can grow from seed.

## Straw Daisy

*Helichrysum* annual

These are brightly coloured flowers in scarlet, orange, pink, yellow and white. Cut the flowers when they are half open and hang in bunches to dry for a few weeks, in a cool, dry, dark place.

## Sea Lavender

*Limonium* perennial

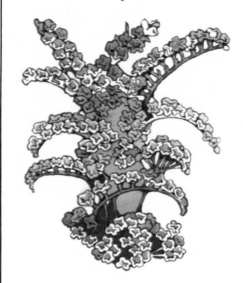

The tiny flowers come in shades of blues and pinks on wide branching sprays. Cut for drying on a sunny day.

## Honesty

*Lunaria* biennial

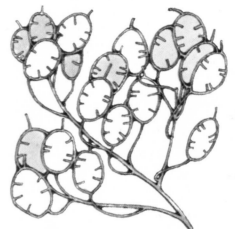

Honesty will flower the year after you sow it. Once it is in your garden, it will seed itself very easily. It is grown for its beautiful silver seed pods. Pick it when you see the silver seed pods. Take off the leaves and hang the seed pods upside down to dry.

## Chinese Lanterns

*Physalis* perennial

When you see the bright orange lanterns on the plants, it is the time to cut the stems. Take off the leaves and hang bunches upside down for drying.

## Achillea

perennial

Achillea is a tall plant with pretty flat flower heads of deep yellow. Cut them for drying when they are in full bloom. Rub off the leaves and hang small bunches up to dry.

## Ripe Seed Heads

Some ripe seed heads of flowers, like poppies and love-in-a-mist, can be picked and used straight away in a dried flower arrangement. They look very pretty painted silver or gold.

# Sprays of leaves to preserve

On nature walks in the country, look for wild plants to keep. Look for teasel, bullrushes, catkins and pussy willows. Bring them home to dry by hanging them upside down in a cool, airy place. Many leaves can be preserved on branches, especially from trees like Beech, Hornbeam, Maple, Laurel, Eucalyptus and Lime [Linden].

**1** Split the base of the woody stems of the branches for 5 or 7.5 cm (2 or 3 in.).

Make a lovely winter flower arrangement in a vase.

**3** Pour the glycerine solution into a narrow container and stand the stems in about 5 cm (2 in.) of the mixture.

**2** Stand the branches in a bucket of warm water for a few hours. If any leaves curl up, throw these stems away as they will not preserve well.

# You Will Need

Branches of leaves

A bucket

A solution of 1 part glycerine to 2 parts of water, boiled together

A narrow container

**4** Put the container into an empty bucket. Allow the branches to soak up the glycerine for several weeks so that it reaches all the leaves.

41

# Use Your Plants

You could press some of the flowers you grow during the year and save them to make pretty Christmas presents.

## Pressing Flowers

## You Will Need

Flowers—choose single rather than double varieties as these press better

Sheets of blotting paper

A large book or flower press

A heavy weight like a brick

**1** Pick the flowers on a sunny day when they are quite dry.

Your flowers will fade in colour during pressing and drying. Bright colours will eventually turn to shades of brown.

**2** Place the flowers between two sheets of blotting paper. Do not let the flowers touch each other.

**3** Put the blotting paper, with the flowers inside, between the leaves of a heavy book or in a flower press.

Place a heavy weight, like a brick, on top of the book, or screw down your flower press. Leave the flowers to press—without looking at them—until you need to use them.

CALENDAR

6 Your calendar is ready to give as a present or to use at home.

## Make a Pressed Flower Calendar

You will want to plan your calendar in advance so that you can collect and press the appropriate flowers as they flower in their seasons. Choose the flowers you are going to press to represent certain months. For the winter months you might choose snowdrops or crocus; for the spring months you could select daffodils or tulips; for the summer months you might use roses and pansies; for the autumn months you could choose michaelmas daisies.

## You Will Need

6 varieties of pressed flowers
    to represent the months
    in which they flower
6 sheets of stiff white card
Clear, sticky-backed plastic sheet
Rubber-based adhesive
Ribbon
Calendar booklet

1 Arrange the pressed flowers on the sheets of white card according to the months they represent to make a pretty design.

2 Dab some adhesive very lightly on the backs of the flowers to stick them down.

3 Cut the clear, sticky-backed plastic sheet into a square or rectangle 2.5 cm (1 in.) larger on all sides than the white card. Very carefully stick it all over the white card and fold over the edges. Remember, once it is in place you cannot remove it.

4 Punch two holes through the top of each card and thread the cards together with ribbon.

5 Attach a calendar to the bottom of the back card with two strips of ribbon.

# Amusing Presents

## You Will Need

A packet of *Luffa* seeds
Plant pot
Compost [potting mixture]

## A Tickly Bathroom Sponge

A loofah is a hard, rough sponge, often used for scrubbing dirty knees
in the bath! You can grow them for yourself. The plant is called *Luffa*.

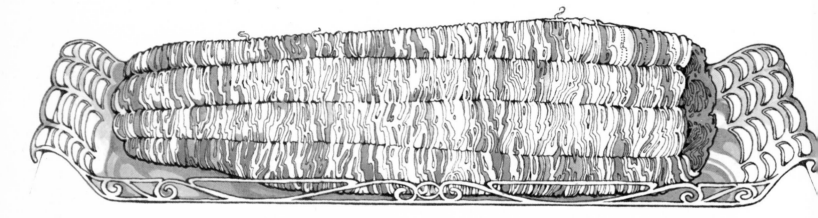

**1** Plant the large black *Luffa* seed in a pot of compost
[potting mixture] in early spring. Keep the pot in a sunny,
warm place.

**2** In a few weeks you should see a tiny cucumber-like plant.
Plant it out in the garden in a light, rich soil. It likes a sunny
spot, sheltered from wind.

**3** By autumn, your *Luffa* plant should have produced
several small loofahs for the bath. Pick them at the end of
the growing season and put them in a warm place to dry out.

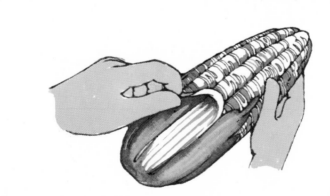

**4** When they are dry, peel off their skins. Inside will be
your new loofahs.

# Gorgeous Gourds (Cucurbita)

Gourds are funny—even when they are growing! They love to spread along the ground, or they will climb up sticks or string. The fruits can be in all sorts of decorative shapes and colours.

## You Will Need

A packet of mixed Cucurbita seeds

Sticks or string

Dry cloth

Clear varnish

Varnish brush

Basket

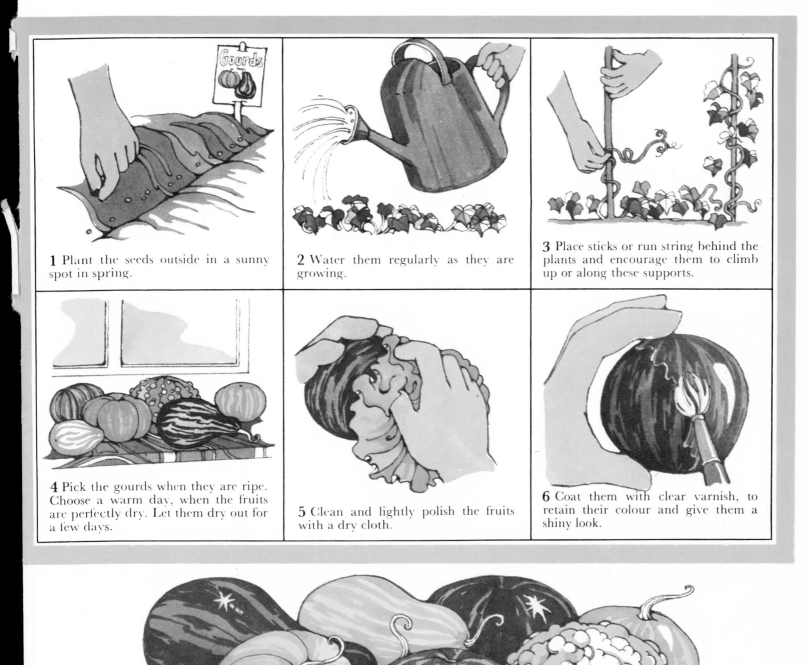

**1** Plant the seeds outside in a sunny spot in spring.

**2** Water them regularly as they are growing.

**3** Place sticks or run string behind the plants and encourage them to climb up or along these supports.

**4** Pick the gourds when they are ripe. Choose a warm day, when the fruits are perfectly dry. Let them dry out for a few days.

**5** Clean and lightly polish the fruits with a dry cloth.

**6** Coat them with clear varnish, to retain their colour and give them a shiny look.

**7** Arrange them in a pretty basket, to make an attractive table decoration.

# Growing Vegetables

## A Wigwam of Runner [Green] Beans

Runner [green] beans take up little space if they are grown on a wigwam frame. They look pretty and will give you several crops in summer.

**1** Put the sticks in the ground at the corners of a small triangle and tie them together at the top to make a wigwam.

**2** Runner [green] beans can be planted when the soil is warm. They will not germinate if it is cold. Wait until late spring to put in your seeds.

**3** Plant one seed on each side of a stick.

**4** As the seedlings grow, encourage them to twine round the sticks.

## You Will Need

Six runner [green] bean seeds
Three tall sticks
String

**5** When the beans begin to flower, spray them with water to help to set the flowers.

**6** Keep picking the beans as they become ready, before the seeds start to swell inside the pods. When you are harvesting the beans look behind the large leaves as they hide behind them. The more beans you pick, the more will grow.

# Two Vegetables from One Plant

## Perpetual Spinach or Seakale Beet

If your family likes spinach, this perpetual variety, known as Silver Beet or Swiss Chard, is easy to grow.

## You Will Need

A packet of Swiss Chard seeds

**1** Sow the seeds in spring. A row or two will be enough to feed the family all summer!

**2** Thin out the seedlings, after a few weeks, so that they are about 20.5 cm (8 in.) apart.

**3** Pull out weeds which grow near the plants.

**4** Cut the stems when they are ready. More will grow quickly.

**5** Ask your mother to cut the leaves for spinach. The stems can be tied in bundles, boiled and served like asparagus.

# Keep a Tree Record

## You Will Need

A young tree
Camera
Measuring tape
Note book

For your next Christmas or birthday present, ask your parents to give you a tree. A record of its growth will be more fun than keeping a diary.

Choose a tree which will grow quickly and look pretty in your garden, or one which will bear fruit.

You can plant your tree between early winter and spring.

Ask your parents to take a photograph of you standing beside your tree.

Measure the height of your tree.

Keep regular details of your tree in a special scrap book. Note down how tall it grows each year and how many fruit it bears.

Each year, on the tree's birthday, have another photograph taken. Then you can compare your rates of growth!